風
水

# Feng Shui

## at home

# Feng Shui

## at home

Carol Soucek King M.F.A. Ph.D.

Distributor to the book trade in the United States
and Canada
Rizzoli International Publications through
St. Martin's Press, 175 Fifth Avenue
New York, NY 10010

Distributor to the art trade in the United States
and Canada
PBC International Inc, One School Street
Glen Cove, NY 11542

Distributor throughout the rest of the world
Hearst Books International
1350 Avenue of the Americas, New York, NY 10019

Library of Congress Cataloging-in-Publication Data
King, Carol Soucek.
Feng Shui at Home / by Carol Soucek King.
    p.   cm.
Includes index.
ISBN 0-86636-639-3  (hardcover).
1. Feng-shui.              I. Title.
BF1779.F4K55  1999              99-9657
133.3'337—dc21
CIP

CAVEAT—
Information  in
this text is believed
accurate, and will pose no
problem for the student or
casual reader. However, the author
was often constrained by information
contained in signed release forms, information
that could have been in error or not included at all.
Any misinformation (or lack of information) is the result
of failure in these attestations. The author has done what-
ever is possible to insure accuracy.       Printed in Hong Kong

10 9 8 7 6 5 4 3 2 1

TO CREATING HOMES IN HARMONY

WITH THE UNIVERSE—AND US!

# Contents

# Preface

Our world today is open to insights about how we may lead better, more sensitive lives—lives attuned to our environment, our heritage our families and ourselves.

Feng shui, which translates literally into "wind/water," views the entire universe and everything in it as interrelated, seeking to emphasize harmony among its various aspects. There are many different approaches to the practice of feng shui, however there are only a few fundamental principles that always apply.

## THE ELEMENTS

The ancients believed that the world is made up of five elements: earth, wood, fire, metal and water. In feng shui today, those five elements—and the colors, forms and other characteristics that symbolize them—continue to be emphasized.

## BALANCE

The main thing is that there should be an appropriate balance among the elements. Of course that appropriateness depends on many things, including the people and purpose the particular environment is to serve.

## DATE ANALYSIS

Feng shui consultants can devote much time to analyzing your birth date, the current date, the date your property was built or remodeled, as well as other time cycles.

## ORDER AND CLEANLINESS

One can scarcely speak about balance without thinking of "order." Along with order comes cleanliness. Both are emphasized again and again in feng shui.

## YIN/YANG

Yin and yang are the two complementary opposites that are expressed in all beings and all things. Yin represents receptive, reflective, passive, feminine qualities. Yang represents active, moving, warm, masculine qualities. Obviously, a combination of both exists in almost everything and everyone. It follows that yin and yang can be expressed in color, shape, lighting and mood.

## CHI

The life force or vital energy of the universe, chi, or "ch'i" must flow easily—not too quickly and not too slowly—throughout a space for its benefits to be optimized. To maintain good chi, one must establish an appropriate balance between nature and manmade structures so that they can coexist in harmony.

## BAGUA

Originating in the ancient Chinese book on divination, the *I Ching*, or "Book of Changes," the bagua map incorporates the eight basic areas important in life. Although the names of those eight areas vary slightly from book to book and teacher to teacher, they are: love, wealth, reputation, health, creativity, knowledge, career and helpfulness. Feng shui consultants use the bagua to help ascertain the placement of a building on the land and the most auspicious placement of areas within for certain activities.

Bagua

Reputation / Fame

Wealth / Prosperity

Love / Commitment

Health / Family

Creativity / Children

Knowledge / Education

Helpful People

Career

# Introduction

Welcome to FENG SHUI at home. It is with exhilaration and joy that I find myself writing at a time when so many people are seeing the designed environment as far more than skin deep.

It is now the exception rather than the rule to think of design as mere fancy. The spiritual aspect of life has become our common denominator. All of us take it for granted that our surroundings are in constant exchange with our inner state; the more we elevate our understanding of how to express that, the more we positively affect our lives and the lives of those around us.

While many books have been published about the principles of feng shui, none have shown the results in such expertly photographed, sensitively wrought homes and gardens. It is for that reason that I am particularly indebted to the PBC International staff for handling this material with the care and the thoughtfulness it deserves.

I am especially indebted to the designers, architects, consultants and clients who have allowed us to share their heartfelt belief in the value of feng shui in contemporary design. Each knew more about the subject than I, yet each entrusted me to carry forth their message.

Last but not least is my gratitude to the many who have contributed their words of wisdom to this book. Several of them have guided me during my attempt to understand this ancient philosophy. Therefore, never-ending fair winds and gently flowing waters to: Alie Chang, Michael Chiang, Terah Kathryn Collins, Cissie Cooper, Kartar Diamond, Miller Yee Fong, Mariãngela Guimarães, Jean-Marie Hamel, Chun-Chia Hwang, Dennis Jenkins, Pamela Laurence, Jami Lin, Carol Olten, Neiva Gessi Rizzotto, Sarah Rossbach, Bonnie Sachs, Teck-Sing Tie, Adele D. Trebil, and Valerie von Sobel. Thank you with all my heart for helping to lead the way!

Carol Soucek King

LOCATION: La Costa, California

SQUARE FEET/METERS: 210/20

DESIGN BUDGET: $65,000

INTERIOR DESIGNER: Valerie von Sobel Interior Design

FENG SHUI CONSULTANT: Terah Kathryn Collins

PHOTOGRAPHY: Mary E. Nichols

For Valerie von Sobel, whose 19-year-old son Andre had just died from a brain tumor, the need for peace and tranquility ran deep.

To quiet her thoughts as well as to commemorate Andre, she transformed his bedroom into a space conducive to the contemplation so important to one seeking inner harmony.

Von Sobel sought inspiration for the sense of sanctuary she wanted in the architecture of the Japanese temple and teahouse. She melded their various elements into her own Western version of an ideal meditation space.

A tranquil space can ease

風水
Please Remove
Your Shoes

*the path to inner harmony.*

The elements of Japanese design that most suited von Sobel's idea of a spiritually grounding space are all here—a calming scale, minimal furnishings, natural materials such as cedar, bamboo and rice paper, an elegantly refined Tokonoma (alcove) and a formal sand and rock garden. Wherever one sits, the eye is invited to rest on a point of calm.

The bed does not have to be stored in the tansu during the day. A footwell has been cut into the ground below the low writing desk, and zaisu (legless chairs), offer back support for those not accustomed to sitting on the floor.

土 In the formal garden, sand, rock and bamboo provide a psychological connection to nature at all times. To create balance between elements, feng shui consultant Terah Kathryn Collins, founder of the Western School of Feng Shui, suggested placing a shallow pool of water and river rocks in front of the fireplace. The protective shape of the bamboo canopy over the bed, situated on an elevated tatami platform, offers a sense of security.

LOCATION: New York, New York

SQUARE FEET/METERS: 591/55

DESIGN BUDGET: not disclosed

ARCHITECT/INTERIOR DESIGNER: Clodagh Design International

FENG SHUI CONSULTANT: Sarah Rossbach

PHOTOGRAPHY: © 1998 Daniel Aubry

"Feng shui, like design, is a healing art," says Clodagh of the continuous thread found throughout her work. To her, design is never a collection of static objects but rather a life-enhancing process that affects body and soul.

This highly intuitive approach, expressed in the Moroccan-inspired bedroom Clodagh designed for the 1998 Kips Bay Boys & Girls Club Decorator Show House, adds layer upon layer of experience to activate the mind and the senses.

Fragrance plays a part. So

Spirits and symbols excite

the mind and the senses

does music. And so does a multiplicity of symbols, a fascinating weave of the five feng shui elements called forth through color, material and form. The result: a deeply meditative space.

"Part of feng shui is most definitely a thought pursuit," says Sarah Rossbach, whose guidance plays a part in all of Clodagh's projects. "Some changes are actually physical. But others that affect only our emotional responses can be just as real.

"The art of feng shui is an act of faith, and faith is such a strong instrument that it can be stronger than any physical cure."

火 Clodagh's evocative layering includes a sumptuous four-poster bed from her home furnishings collection, ensconced in a saturated blue niche and strewn with sensual satins and silks. The stacked wooden rings of the bed's tapered posts echo other primitive shapes—olive presses that serve as bedside tables, an ancient Nepalese oxcart wheel hung as wall sculpture, and an Indonesian chest to hold blankets or television. A vivid green grass ledge brings the outside indoors. Two suspended rock crystals circulate chi. Candles and up-lighting relieve oppression and create liveliness. Clodagh creates the feeling of bathing outdoors by concealing the overhead lighting behind a wood-slatted ceiling so the effect is of sun shining through an outdoor pavilion. Daylight is also simulated by a vast glowing sconce from her lighting collection. The cast concrete bathtub and brushed stainless steel faucet, resting on a limestone slab that has an indented grid filled with small, cream-colored beach stones, further emphasizes the feeling of being surrounded by nature.

LOCATION: **La Jolla, California**

SQUARE FEET/METERS: **900/84**

DESIGN BUDGET: **$10,000**

INTERIOR DESIGNER: **Carol Olten**

PHOTOGRAPHY: **Carol Olten**
**Jerry Rife**

When the fog blows in, the ancient pine trees in the park by Carol Olten's house seem especially mystical, evocative of things unseen. That is just the feeling that drew Olten to her 1917 cottage by the sea.

Built as a writer's retreat and dubbed "The Dreamery," its ethereal quality today wings forth via Olten's poetical interweaving of natural light with a profusion of white paint, white gauze and space enhancing mirrors. The dreaminess is enhanced by her imaginative mix of furnishings, including a dramatic crystal chandelier.

Mystical places fill the

world with tranquility.

feng shui did not serve as Olten's ultimate bible, but its ideas inspired her. To bring nature indoors. To juxtapose bursts of color with all the white and thus balance the five feng shui elements and their yin and yang qualities. To place the furniture for protection, especially in the bedroom. Most important, to cultivate mystery, illusion and simplicity.

As Olten suggests, "Mystery, mystical places—indeed, the white beast—that is what the world of spirit is about. N'est pas?"

金 A deep blue fireplace surround and a strategically placed mirror reflect the home's oneness with nature. An infinity of white paint uplifts the sequestered feeling of the living area, as do the bright lemon yellow at the windows and the sheen of the gilded appointments. In the spirit of feng shui and designing with spirituality in mind, Olten has used many small mirrors and one large crystal chandelier to add illusion, magic and visual mystery—as well as to visually enlarge the 900-square-foot space.

金 The master bedroom is mystical and minimal, with white painted floors, walls and ceiling, white bed linens, and eggshell-white silk organza curtains also used in the bathroom. There are only two pieces of furniture in the room: an antique rope bed and antique English table/nightstand with ivory inlay. The bed is placed at an angle to face the staircase for protective vigilance, and to ensure peaceful dreams in this respite designed for the cultivation of the imagination.

LOCATION: Philadelphia, Pennsylvania

SQUARE FEET/METERS: 1,500/139

DESIGN BUDGET: not disclosed

INTERIOR DESIGNER: Floss Barber Inc.

PHOTOGRAPHY: Jeff Totaro

Innately sensitive to things unseen, interior designer Floss Barber not only knows but feels her apartment's auspicious history, located in an 1860s residence given to its builder's granddaughter as a wedding present. The generosity of that gift, the kindness reminding Barber of her own father and grandfather, envelops Barber daily with a sense of well-being.

Her apartment's well-proportioned and square main rooms facilitate positive chi. Its 13-foot-high ceilings provide a feeling of wealth and generosity. Its

Past, present, future—

connected, ever moving.

水 To counterbalance the exterior's red brick, which disproportionately emphasizes its yang qualities in comparison to adjacent buildings, the apartment's ceilings are painted yin-enhancing pink and blue. The long entry corridor's tendency to choke chi energy is offset with mirrors, plants and a crystal-laden light. In the living room, an eclectic mix of old and new furnishings, cool and warm colors, soft and hard materials and round and angular shapes balance yin and yang qualities. Red accents help to counterbalance the room's predominance of wood. In the bedroom, mirrors and a firecracker are used to activate chi energy at two poorly positioned doors. A Tibetan *tonka,* denoting protection, and a Czech artwork, representing good fortune and Barber's ancestry, are placed in the corner determined to be the apartment's favorable career position. A Robert Younger sculpture represents Yoga's seven chakra energy centers, with the top lit for enlightenment. The pastel colors and circular motif of the painted ceiling encompass the entire room with a peaceful yin feeling.

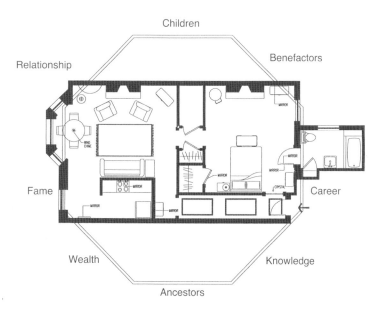

predominant wood and earth elements are believed to support her own personal energy, determined to be metal. While the apartment falls partially in the shadow of taller buildings nearby, the disadvantages are mitigated since its own peaked facade is thought to enhance residents' individuality.

Nevertheless, certain aspects did need readjustment to ensure full expression of the apartment's affirmative characteristics. Each one was handled through Barber's understanding of feng shui and her own intuitive feeling for design as a powerful influence on our mental as well as physical well-being.

LOCATION: Playa del Rey, California

SQUARE FEET/METERS: 3,500/326

DESIGN BUDGET: not disclosed

INTERIOR DESIGNER/FENG SHUI CONSULTANT: Bonnie Sachs, ASID-
Interior Design & Feng Shui

PHOTOGRAPHY: Weldon Brewster

When new owners move into an existing property, the task is often to harmonize all the previous remodels. This home, while lovely, offered a major challenge.

The overly-bright front windows needed adjustable shutters. The previously blocked flow of chi in the sharply-angular family room was alleviated by a curved fireplace/audio/video cabinet and by the rounded upholstered pieces.

To further the out-of-doors connection, french doors were added. The only fabrics used are natural—cotton, linen and wool. To

A home should envelop one

with a sense of well-being.

風 Integrating the home with nature, sandstone in the breakfast room flows seamlessly to the pool deck. The placement of the swimming pool adjacent to living areas alleviates the need for water features in the interior. In the bedroom, a canopy bed helps to cancel negative energy inherent in the overhead beam.

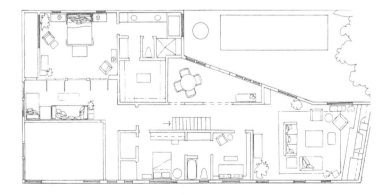

strengthen the balance of yin and yang, the use of Asian cabinets imbue the otherwise modern space with a sense of depth and history.

Since the entire house has overhead beams, the furniture has been situated to draw the eye away from these potentially oppressive elements.

Finally, collectibles have been used with abandon. A flexible, inexpensive way to ensure the presence of all five elements, art and artifacts can correct a home's flaws and at the same time reflect its occupants' vitality.

LOCATION: Miami, Florida

SQUARE FEET/METERS: 3,000/279

DESIGN BUDGET: not disclosed

INTERIOR DESIGNER: Earth Design

FENG SHUI CONSULTANT: Jami Lin

PHOTOGRAPHY: Barry J. Grossman Photography

When remodeling her home, author/interior designer/feng shui consultant Jami Lin found that she needed to create a more profound balance between structure and site. Her answer was to add an inviting exterior living space that harmoniously connects house, pool and chikee, an open-thatched hut made of wood and palm fronds in the tradition of Indians native to south florida.

Serving as both entry and gathering place, this space provides a long, nurturing breath of chi along the transition between exterior and interior worlds.

Wrap your home in the

nurturing arms of chi.

木 From humorous mementos to more formal works of art, every item in the house is valued for its symbolic meaning. So too is the layout of the rooms and their relationship to each other and the out-of-doors—the offices (yang) are on one side of the living room or heart of the home, and the master bedroom (yin) along with the nurturing master bath and kitchen are on the other side. The entry courtyard with its fountain of water is located near the master bedroom, believed to be an auspicious location for enabling water to energize abundant helpfulness.

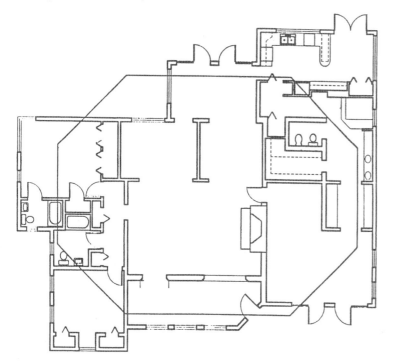

Inside, rooms are spacious and inviting. Furnishings and accessories are positioned to further direct chi so that it is guided into all areas. "If it catches your eye, it alters chi," says the designer.

Lin has selected relatively neutral, earth-related colors and finishes, to neutralize the fire and wood type personalities of herself and her husband. As life experiences change the couple's personal energies, Lin further refines the composition by adding or deleting any of the five elements and their symbolic colors by her use of accessories. "Possessions," she teaches, "should be no more static than life."

LOCATION: Los Angeles, California

SQUARE FEET/METERS: 5,500/511

DESIGN BUDGET: not disclosed

INTERIOR DESIGNER: J.F. Chen Antiques

PHOTOGRAPHY: Martin Fine Photography

Antiques dealer/designer Joel Chen has feng shui in his bones, yet he ignored it until the recent renovation of his family's Los Angeles home.

"The older you get, the more you realize the importance of deeply understanding everything you do," he says. "I have always believed that everything is connected, so in renovating my home I wanted to pay more attention to that feeling through feng shui. The notion of renovation is completely in line with feng shui—making everything clean and bright."

Everything is connected

in the journey of life.

There are difficulties, of course. "When feng shui conflicts with one's interior design ideas, it's not easy," he notes. "You have to work out the whole aesthetics."

This means combining one's design sense with the interplay of the five feng shui elements and their yin and yang manifestations, the changing cycles—and even the birthdays and stars of everyone living in the home.

"To truly understand feng shui takes a lifetime," Chen concludes. "Much is common sense—like flowers bringing joy to a room—but other things are more subtle. I feel I'm just getting started."

土 A partially dissolved "scholar's rock" dispels danger. In the living room, a J.F. Chen reproduction mirror reflects positive energy and a bronze mobile provides fluidity. An 18th-century Portuguese cabinet supports a Sino-Tibetan arnhat, its gilded bronze suggesting liveliness. The painting's predominant round shape denotes righteousness and circulation. Another view of the study shows a Buddha, connoting harmony, as well as a screen depicting cranes, for happiness and grace.

土 The desk and two jade brushes
face north, a good position for
the educational/intellectual star.
The mirror absorbs good and deflects evil;
its round shape brings good fortune and
righteousness. The stone monkey denotes
energy and good fortune. The Ming jar is
harmonious with the blue-and-white vase;
in Chinese, the word "vase" is a phonetic
synonym for the word "peace." The
Prosperity Bamboo's height symbolizes
aspiration. The master bedroom's desk
also faces north to capture the good
rays of the intellectual star.

LOCATION: Cherry Hill, New Jersey

SQUARE FEET/METERS: 5,000/465

DESIGN BUDGET: not disclosed

INTERIOR DESIGNER: Mitchell J. Rubin Associates, Inc.

PHOTOGRAPHY: Wade Zimmerman

Invited to custom design this home inside and out, designer Mitchell Rubin did not have to compromise—and it shows. Every inch has been molded into the clear vision he and his clients had of a sparse, calm, deeply sensitive living space.

The main space is separated into three areas for dining, living and study. This is achieved via the placement of a highly edited collection of furnishings—a sort of floating premise that promotes the flow of chi. The three areas are further indicated by the column placement and, in

Real luxury comes from

deeply sensitive design.

the foyer, by the floor pattern.

Scale and proportion were especially important. Rubin used a square—in feng shui a manifestation of the earth element—used as his basic building block. The dimensions of the great room and foyer are precise multiples of a ten-foot square.

The ceiling heights frame a spatial geometry that creates a soothing atmosphere. The great room's sloped ceiling soars from 10 to 17 feet; it is balanced by the feng shui solution of opposing forms—the vertical wall above the two columns and the ten-foot foyer ceiling.

LOCATION: **Pacific Palisades, California**

SQUARE FEET/METERS: **6,300/585**

DESIGN BUDGET: **not disclosed**

INTERIOR DESIGNER: **Cissie Cooper Design Services**

FENG SHUI CONSULTANTS: **Nathan V. Batoon**
**Katherine Metz**
**Roy Anthony Shabla**

PHOTOGRAPHY: **Martin Fine Photography**

When Cissie Cooper first suggested using feng shui to the owner of this hilltop Mediterranean-style residence, he rolled his eyes and said "Forget it!" Two days later, however, after seeing Donald Trump rave about feng shui on Cable News Network (CNN), he told Cooper to go ahead.

In the end, masters from three different schools of feng shui were consulted. They informed him and his wife that certain structural elements of the house posed serious threats to their well-being, including the soaring height of the ceilings which, if not

Design—a Wellspring

for spiritual evolution.

corrected, could allow chi to dissipate rather than circulate. By then the clients were not only eager to execute all the remedies but also to use feng shui as Cooper does—as part of one's spiritual evolution and self-mastery.

Today the couple enjoy the process of accumulating a collection of furniture, art and antiques even as they experience the rejuvenating powers of the house in all aspects of their lives. Rather than emphasizing design as a material, physical thing, they are focusing on the concepts of expansiveness, lighthearted-ness and transformation.

金 In a hallway, the painting's distant horizon line, a potted plant representing a field of flowers and a winged torso's sense of freedom stimulate the movement of stagnant, blocked chi. The living room's disproportionately high ceiling, which dissipated chi, was alleviated by the low placement of the heavy drapery rods and the chandeliers. Whimsical wood pieces bring energy to the family room. Since the dining room is directly opposite the main entry, a low chandelier, the strength of the stone table and the placement of an antique tapestry prevent chi from rushing out the French doors.

金 The master bath is a complex in microcosm of the five elements as they relate to the rest of the house, each element and remedy represented in the appropriate place on the bagua plan. Everything was placed with intention and prayer. The powder room, located in the bagua love and relationships area, features sconces with a man and woman making eye contact across the vast universe of a mirror. Positive attributes in this earth-element room are enhanced by four candles.

LOCATION: Southern California

SQUARE FEET/METERS: 3,800/353

DESIGN BUDGET: not disclosed

ARCHITECT/INTERIOR DESIGNER : Hiatt Enterprises International, Inc.

PHOTOGRAPHY: Charles White Photography

This home was completed before its review by two feng shui masters, but no matter. Nothing needed to be changed.

The designer, Douglas Pierce Hiatt, was not surprised. "Feng shui is about aligning a space with universal energy," he says. "Well, this is the way I've always designed intuitively."

While not actually planned with the guidance of feng shui, Hiatt's design does invite a quiet, thoughtful attitude. Furthermore, he achieved it via a harmonious balance of feng shui's five building blocks, the

Enlightened design is more

than the sum of its parts.

elements necessary for any unified physical environment.

Predominant is water, beginning with the entry pool. In feng shui, glass, mirror and other reflective surfaces symbolize water.

Metal is represented by actual metals, such as gold, and by stones, the color white, and round shapes.

Fire is represented by subtle lighting effects and by actual fireplaces.

Wood is present in carved furnishings. In feng shui, natural materials, plants and even columns, refer to trees.

Earth is represented by the extensive use of horizontal planes.

水 The entry's polychrome Buddha in a lushly planted pool instills a sense of welcoming calm that continues throughout the residence to the indoor/outdoor spa. Soft shapes, relaxed furniture placements and beveled edges promote the feeling of ease, safety and smoothly flowing energy. Other nurturing aspects—such as protective planted areas immediately outside the windows, a curved privacy wall behind the spa, and a coromandel screen in front of a long straight line of closet doors—keep chi from passing through too quickly.

LOCATION: São Paulo, Brazil

SQUARE FEET/METERS: 5,380/500

DESIGN BUDGET: $500,000

ARCHITECT/INTERIOR DESIGNER: Studio Arthur de Mattos Casas

FENG SHUI CONSULTANT: Lourdes Machado

PHOTOGRAPHY: Tuca Reinés

Since this home is located near a beautiful park in the middle of São Paulo, the goal was to create a feeling of interaction with the exterior so that the people within can at all times connect to the city and nature beyond.

Also, the owners expressed their desire that the house reflect an atmosphere of peace and serenity. Their feng shui consultant suggested that the rooms be designed so that the five elements might reflect throughout a harmonious relationship with the universe.

To emphasize earth, the walls and flooring are wood. The

Good design evokes a

universal connection.

basically off-white color palette is accented by earth-suggestive hues of green and brown. A tree, cut flowers and rectangular shapes further ground the design in evocations of earth.

Warm lights and candles bring in the element of fire. Mirrors, glass cabinets and shades that mitigate nature's light with a welcome translucence enhance the sense of spaciousness. The energy of water is suggested through certain curved elements—such as the design of a carpet, a stool and the armchairs. While not visually apparent, metal is present in the construction.

風 Wood, glass, color, light, earthily-rectangular forms juxtaposed with softly rounded edges, reflective materials and living plants—all five elements of the universe are combined in harmony. Even the collection of art deco sculptures by Chiparvs and Preiss are placed in a glass cabinet that not only divides living and dining areas but also transmits the feeling of light and air. All surfaces made of plastic laminate have been painted to void the un-natural feeling. Shades made of wood and natural fabrics diffuse light without blocking the feeling of being connected to nature.

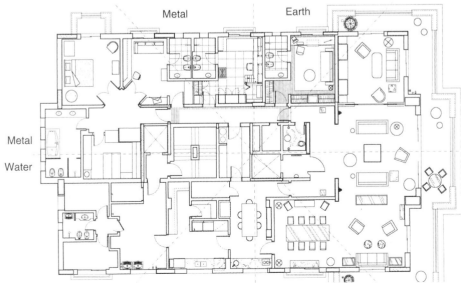

LOCATION: Monterey, California

SQUARE FEET/METERS: 1,200/117

DESIGN BUDGET: not disclosed

INTERIOR DESIGNER: Maxcy Design

FENG SHUI CONSULTANT: Seann Xenja

PHOTOGRAPHY: © Russell Abraham 1998
© Marco Zecchin

"According to feng shui, we should never have given this house a second look," says designer Donald Maxcy. "But it was those irregularities and idiosyncrasies that told us we could be comfortable here."

To be sure, Maxcy and Marsha, his wife and partner, combined the insights of feng shui with their own ideas. It was a perfect match, with the Maxcys' aesthetic sense and the master's advice in total harmony.

Narrow siting previously necessitated steep steps leading up to the glass front door. The

Homes should be poetry

— no more, no less.

situation was dangerous, and also blasted chi energy into the house. Thus informed, the Maxcys acquired some adjacent land, which allowed them to realize their dream of a bamboo garden that orchestrates a truly graceful flow of chi. Guests tend to enter more eloquently as well.

The visual welcome continues in every room, with the collection of art, furnishings and decorative elements placed according to the tenets of feng shui as well as the owners' elevated sensibilities.

木 In the living area, Michael Brangoccio's strongly red "Announcement" repels negative elements. An oversized bamboo chair enables the owners to oversee the entry. The dining room's ill-fated shape—narrowing toward the back window/wall and allowing chi to rush through—has been remedied by a woven bamboo screen and a decorative bone mirror hung to reflect the view. In the guest bedroom, where clerestory windows over the bed disturbed tranquility, a wall-size tapestry has been hung to nurture the privacy within.

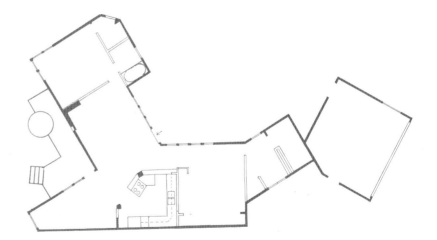

LOCATION: Tokyo, Japan

SQUARE FEET/METERS: 4,400/409

DESIGN BUDGET: not disclosed

ARCHITECT: Hiroshi Mishiru

LIGHTING DESIGNER: Motoko Ishii Lighting Design Inc.

FENG SHUI CONSULTANT: Shuganshi Hidetada Takahashi

PHOTOGRAPHY: Yoichi Yamazaki
Misawa Homes Co., Ltd.

How perfect that the well-known lighting designer Motoko Ishii would arrange her Tokyo home over her new MIOS showroom. Located in Nishi-Azabu, one of Tokyo's most fashionable areas, it is convenient for customers as well as for Ishii's husband, a professor of law, and daughter, also a lighting designer. The feeling of nature, however, had to be provided entirely through the palette of materials, colors and potted plants because the lot is surrounded by buildings.

No matter. It was determined

Light is life from

beginning to end.

that moving to the new house would be positive for all members of the family—as long as certain directives were followed. They included: that the house be strong in form, that each person in the family have his or her own space, and that plants and water elements be used to compensate for the home's arid southern exposure.

The spiritual consultant also advised that the terrace be made to feel more expansive and welcoming. Above all, he suggested warm off-white and wood tones to help integrate the home with the nature and light so essential to this family's well-being.

土 Glass block creates the look of shoji screens in the entrance hall. Warm colors—ranging from off-white to beige with touches of orange—provide a relaxing, uplifting atmosphere. A Buddhist altar is located on a shelf, and, for the display of art, a large white wall replaces the traditional Tokonoma alcove. A glass roof and wide windows allow the terrace to be used year-round.

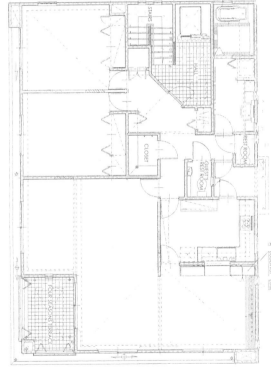

土 Light, candles and growing trees turn the terrace into a gathering place suitable for friends as well as family, one of the home's many aspects suggested by the feng shui compass. In a bedroom, small square windows represent the nine energy centers of the bagua map and illuminate the touches of yellow and orange that enforce the development of life and health. Green plants immediately outside promote the flow of natural energy without blocking the sun.

LOCATION: **Santa Monica, California**

SQUARE FEET/METERS: **5,500/511**

DESIGN BUDGET: **$500,000**

INTERIOR ARCHITECT: **Alie Design Inc.**

PHOTOGRAPHY: **Mary E. Nichols**

Abundant with surprise, delight, nature and creativity, this home celebrates living in harmony with the elements, with oneself and with one's family and friends.

Framed by flowers and tropical ferns, the hillside villa rises from courtyard to terrace to balcony to roof garden. Each level reaches out toward carefully framed vistas and restful alcoves. Koi ponds, waterfalls and even a small indoor fern grotto refresh many areas. Fireplaces and sunny exposures warm others. All are illuminated with light modulated by skylights, windows and glass.

*High as the Wind*

and deep as the sea.

火 The back of the home is hugged by a hillside that provides support, while its location at the canyon's mouth enables its view side to be spacious enough so as not to block chi. Colors are borrowed from earth tones—peach-beige clay, off-white limestone, dusty rose granite and deep green slate. The balanced lighting is achieved by carefully placed windows, skylights and glass block, lending to each room a greenhouse effect. Works of art, many by Chang herself, are placed freely throughout the house for personal enjoyment.

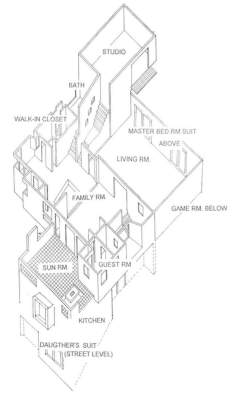

STUDIO

BATH

WALK-IN CLOSET

MASTER BED RM SUIT

ABOVE

LIVING RM.

FAMILY RM.

GAME RM. BELOW

SUN RM.    GUEST RM

KITCHEN

DAUGTHER'S SUIT
(STREET LEVEL)

As a child, interior architect Alie Chang absorbed an understanding of feng shui from her architect father without conscious effort. The ideas of feng shui filtered through her belief system as if by osmosis. They inform her design today in the same way—without deliberation but with highly sensitive, deeply felt intuition.

No wonder this haven inspires and sustains Chang, her husband and their daughter. Likewise, two feng shui masters visiting from China found the home conducive to health and prosperity.

LOCATION: New York, New York

SQUARE FEET/METERS: 2,200/204

DESIGN BUDGET: $350,000

INTERIOR DESIGNER: Laura Bohn Design Associates.

FENG SHUI CONSULTANT: Master Pun Yin

PHOTOGRAPHY: Michael Dunne

Many of us seek help from feng shui as a last resort. That was the way it was when designer Laura Bohn was trying to solve the problems she and her husband were having with their new loft space.

"So many things were going wrong and I didn't know where else to turn," says Bohn. "So I called a client's feng shui consultant, thinking I should try this myself."

With just one look, Master Pun Yin was able to pinpoint numerous negative energy sources—the trash compactor located outside the front door, a neighboring

Healing the home is medi

cine for one's entire life.

building's brick wall blocking the flow of chi, an immediately adjacent parking lot producing negative energy, a heavy beam over a bed, a desk facing the wrong direction.

Much of Bohn's calming, nurturing design did pass muster. However, once the feng shui healing process was complete, Bohn says that the problems she was having disappeared as easily as the chi energy now flowed in!

金 In the living room, tall ivy plants and large-scale art representing nature counteract negative energy from an adjacent parking lot. In the kitchen, metal cabinetry and stone flooring balance heat and water elements. Seating is not provided around the island, because it also contains the stove—not a power spot according to feng shui. In the master bedroom a hefty headboard pushes the bed away from the wall and the weight of its overhead beam while blinds and metal picture frames further deflect negative energy. To promote marital happiness and compensate for the poor location of the bathroom, round shapes and a soothing color palette were used.

LOCATION: **Carmel Highlands, California**

SQUARE FEET/METERS: **3,900/363**

DESIGN BUDGET: **not disclosed**

ARCHITECT: **Fletcher + Hardoin**

INTERIOR DESIGNER: **Maxcy Design**

PHOTOGRAPHY: **Ron Starr**

Donald Maxcy considers this residence a high point in his design career. It reflects his training at the Rudolph Schaeffer School, his experience as an artist and his 30-plus years in design, as well as his interpretation of his client's desire for simplicity.

In enlarging an existing property to create a second home for his client, a single, very private woman, Maxcy explored his feeling about how the client should experience her residence—freely, creatively, as a nurturing, calming space. He achieved this by using a highly edited selection of

Strip one's walls, one's life

...of all but essentials.

large-scale furnishings. Soft colors and materials reflect the house's coastal site. Skillful interweaving of the client's treasured pieces of furniture with custom designs emphasizes, rather than competes with, the home's magnificent ocean view.

The richness of ritual is present. The mirror installed at the entry's glass doors deflects chi energy from entering too quickly. The circular metal gong in front of the mirror announces guests, symbolically protecting the house from harm.

水 The entry flows into a large rectangular living room overlooking the ocean.

A custom, curved sectional sofa and granite table on a thick shag carpet define the area facing the fireplace, creating an intimate area within the larger space. The curved shapes soften some of the hard angles of the architecture, thus balancing the home's yin/yang, or feminine/masculine, elements. Large bamboo plants frame and retain the chi energy from escaping out the windows. The custom metal bed faces the door, thus protecting the occupant from surprises. The windows' height provides an enormity of ocean and landscape views. Thick foliage offers privacy without the use of drapes. The bedroom contains an abundance of contrasts—metal bed, sumptuous comforters and pillows, gauze bedhangings.

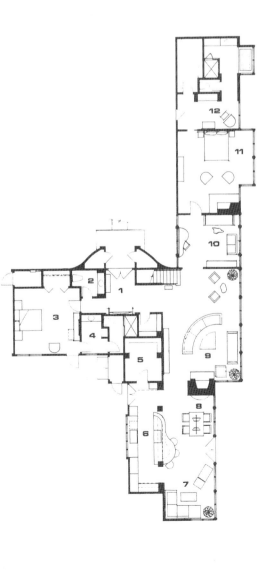

LOCATION: **São Paulo, Brazil**

SQUARE FEET/METERS: **2,411/224**

DESIGN BUDGET: **$30,000**

ARCHITECT/INTERIOR DESIGNER: **Neiva Rizzotto**

FENG SHUI CONSULTANT: **Paulo Lin**

LANDSCAPE ARCHITECT: **Neiva Rizzotto**

PHOTOGRAPHY: **Ricardo de Vicq de Cumptich
Mauricio Simonetti**

Neiva Rizzotto was surprised to find that about eighty percent of her home was in harmony with the principles of feng shui—even though she had designed it years before she studied the ancient Chinese art.

"This demonstrates the intuitive aspect of feng shui, which is very important for someone who wants to practice it," she says.

Yet she did need to organize the twenty percent that was out of balance, especially in terms of the bagua map. Following its guidelines, she enriched the home's career area (water/black)

Nature & intuition, our

guides to a higher state.

with various water elements, including a fountain that represents a lion's head. In the children/creativity area (white), with open spaces that could have challenged family relationships, she added abundant light. In the dining room, located in the fame/reputation area (red), she used appropriate hues. In the wealth/prosperity area (purple/blue/red), she applied different shades of purple. The fireplace was relocated to the fame area, whose very symbol is fire, from the wealth/prosperity area, which was sealed with cinnabar.

風 The career side of the house was enriched with the feng shui element of water and plants that easily sway to and fro in the breeze. In the room which houses the people/travel area, an altar emphasizes an atmosphere of respect, devotion, ceremony and ritual. Bold strokes of the colors symbolizing this area—white, gray and black—are set against a welcoming glow of bright yellow, denoting earth and in tune with the view.

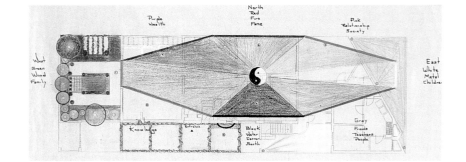

風 On the side of the house representing health and family, the appropriately symbolic color of green is brought in with an abundance of exterior and interior vegetation. In this area, a patio is host to a glass-topped table used to serve lunch and informal dinners. Beyond is a pond enlivened with numerous carp. The quiet retreat for study and meditation is located in the bagua map's knowledge/self-cultivation area (blue/ black/green), for Rizzotto is ever, as she says, "thirsty for knowledge."

LOCATION: **Philadelphia, Pennsylvania**

SQUARE FEET/METERS: **6,000/557**

DESIGN BUDGET: **not disclosed**

INTERIOR DESIGNER: **Floss Barber Inc.**

PHOTOGRAPHY: **Catherine Tighe Bogert**
**Tom Crane**
**Jeff Totaro**

This couple had everything: an elegant residence located in Society Hill and high-powered, successful careers. What they lacked was a sense of warmth and relaxation at home.

There were many positive features to the house: the grand two-story height of the living room and the structure's long and narrow proportions happily suggested the element of tree energy appropriate to the couple's strong career and fame signs. However, despite its luxury and good fit, the house overall did not nourish their spirits.

The life unexamined is

scarcely worth living.

Designer Floss Barber analyzed the reasons. The "oak" floors and casings were in fact plastic. The fireplace was a monolith with a circle at the top, letting all the chi energy escape. A window and door at the end of the galley-type kitchen dissipated chi in that room as well. For all its fine points, including treasured works of art and keepsakes from the couple's frequent trips, the house had no feeling of stability.

Extensive remodeling, refinishing and the use of color, texture, art and lighting have created a place of nurturing comfort.

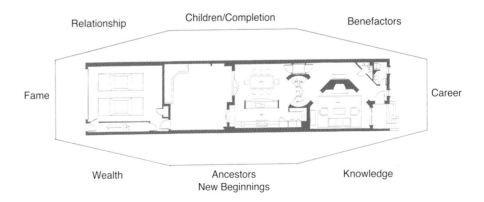

Relationship     Children/Completion     Benefactors

Fame

Career

Wealth     Ancestors
New Beginnings     Knowledge

木 In the living room, a mixture of antiques, comfortable furniture and mahogany stain on floors and trim creates an inviting feeling of stability. The wall in the new beginning, or ancestor, position of the bagua is filled with images of ancient places. The walls of the spiral stair and adjacent rooms were painted Tai Chi yellow, which symbolizes the element of earth to lend a grounding effect. Bright colors and patterns energize the media/ entertainment room. The arrangement of a collection on an illuminated shelf creates a sense of order. A traditional multipaned window replaced the kitchen's former door and window, which let the chi escape too quickly instead of recirculating. To create a communal atmosphere, the kitchen was opened to the dining room. Floors were stained dark and yellow sandstone incorporated to weight the area's yin aspect. A stainless steel stove reflects the burners to enhance wealth. At the stair, a Fortuny light spreads the flow of chi.

LOCATION: Diamond Bar, California

SQUARE FEET/METERS: 7,000/650

DESIGN BUDGET: not disclosed

ARCHITECT: Steven Ehrlich Architects

INTERIOR DESIGNER: Luis Ortega Design Studio

FENG SHUI CONSULTANT : Chun-Chia Hwang

PHOTOGRAPHY: Grey Crawford
Tim Street-Porter

Built for a Taiwanese couple by a California architect and designer in consultation with the couple's feng shui master, this temple-like residence pays homage to the traditions of both East and West.

The influence of feng shui master Chun-Chia Hwang can be seen in the notable union of the two cultures. Architect Steven Ehrlich followed Hwang's feng shui tenets, basing the entire layout of the house on the feng shui bagua. Ehrlich scrapped the idea of placing a swimming pool at a distance from the house when Hwang

How do East and West

meet? Cou t e Ways!

deemed it unpropitious to the site. Instead, he placed a koi pond near the boundaries of the structure. In addition, doors and windows were realigned, and forms and materials selected to maintain Hwang's recommended balance of yin and yang.

Since all such recommendations were made before the structure was built, it seems as if this home was designed from one unified perspective. Because everyone involved believed in the harmonious flow of energy through form, line, material, color and placement, it was.

土 The exterior's massive sheltering roof and prominent eaves give way to an exposed truss ceiling soaring 32 feet over a central hall. Cherry moldings accentuate horizontal, calming, lines. Doors never face each other because the feng shui master advised that they should open instead onto blank walls. The staircase points away from the entry to keep the flow of chi circulating within the house rather than flying out the door.

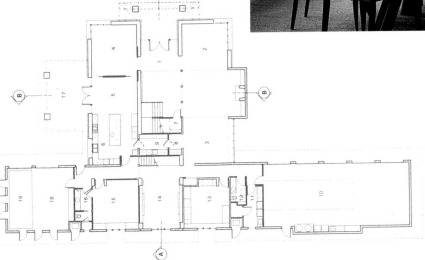

LOCATION: New York, New York

SQUARE FEET/METERS: 3,300/307

DESIGN BUDGET: not disclosed

ARCHITECT/INTERIOR DESIGNER: David Ling Architect

PHOTOGRAPHY: © 1996 Todd Eberle

The style of David Ling's architecture derives from his life's multicultural infusions—nurtured in the United States, formed in Germany, with an umbilical cord still attached to China. His work's distinction, however, comes from his ability to reduce them all to one highly clarified vision.

For example, a single decisive stroke made this urban apartment feel lighter, airier and more spacious. Walls along one side of its 3,300-foot length were blown away, leaving a long, window-abundant space for den, living, dining and kitchen areas. Yet,

# Choreographing opposites

in a dance of tension.

there is no straight view through.

The effect has been achieved via deftly articulated cabinetry. Of variously-sized dimensions with plenty of open space so as not to block the light, the cabinets not only make possible the element of visual surprise but also orchestrate the clients' ceramic and fiber collection into one coherent composition.

Ling's choreography of opposites—industrial with handcrafted, light with dark, curved with straight, the five elements and ying and yang qualities—achieves a calm as soul-fulfilling as if steeped in his Eastern heritage for millennia.

火 Cobalt blue tile, its color and fluid form symbolizing water, is located along the base of the cabinetry and culminates in a large 10-by 10-foot wall behind the breakfast niche. The contrast of the hand-cut, hand-poured tile with the steel plate used elsewhere is dramatic. The dining room's floating chandelier of hand-sanded plexiglass also shows the strokes of human endeavor on industrial materials. To balance the energy from an already early-rising couple, the bedroom is oriented toward the west. The doors and wall panels form a musical rhythm, juxtaposed against the curvaceous contours of the chairs' feminine/yin form. This, the master bedroom, forms the inner private core at the southwest corner of the floor. Shoji screen panels conceal storage, as well as structural elements that could not be removed.

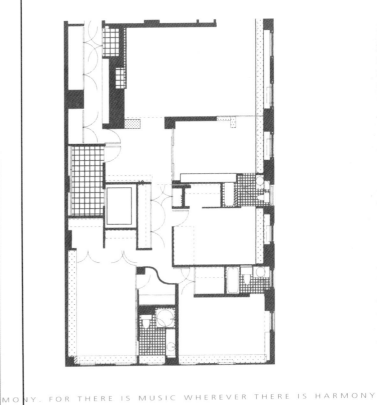

MONY, FOR THERE IS MUSIC WHEREVER THERE IS HARMONY.

LOCATION: Escondido, California

SQUARE FEET/METERS: 6,300/585

DESIGN BUDGET: $45,000

ARCHITECT : Thoryk Architecture, Inc.

INTERIOR DESIGNER: Cheryl Rice Interiors

PHOTOGRAPHY: Campos Photography, Inc.

Although we may not be consciously aware of it, the concept underlying feng shui—that there is a universal connection between everything and every being—is fundamental to many of the finest examples of good design.

Interior designer Cheryl Rice had always known that a room influences far more than just the aesthetics of her clients' lives. "One must remember that everything is alive with energy," she says. "Therefore we should be surrounded by things that support us in our daily life and give us a sense of well-being."

Real sight is illumined by

*the spirit and the soul.*

Yet it was only when designing this home, a custom-designed high-tech showcase house, that she felt drawn to study the ancient Chinese philosophy.

"As I sought to honor nature and the Native American culture, feng shui's definitions of feminine and masculine (yin and yang) attributes and the five universal elements helped me to achieve the sense of nurturing balance I wanted," she says.

The result is a soulful interplay of opposites—and of water, fire, earth, metal and wood elements—that offers far more than just visual satisfaction.

金 Many feminine (yin) characteristics have been used to balance the home's massive (yang) aspects. Corners of interior walls are bullnosed, fabrics are textured and furnishings have rounded lines. The carpet was designed to reflect the home's architecture, its curves mimicking the floor plan and the squares the glass block. Even the Australian limestone has softly curved markings. Topping off the designer's reflection of life's unified, energetic flow are two paintings she commissioned, one of a proud Indian chief, the other of a celebratory dance. More yin features balancing the architecture's strong yang associations include the stairwell's ornate iron and copper railing and banisters with intricate hand-forged depictions of tree limbs and leaves. The same pattern was used for the chandelier, which is further enlivened by natural Brazilian quartz crystals. In the gourmet kitchen, a mural artist simulated the European-style bird's-eye maple cabinetry on the soffit above the island. The architecture itself, while masculine in scale, provides a gentler aspect by following the natural flow of the land.

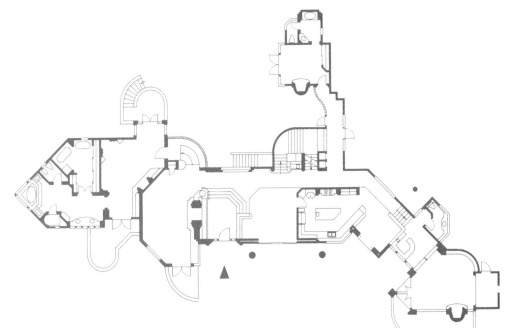

LOCATION: Miami, Florida

SQUARE FEET/METERS: 6,800/632

DESIGN BUDGET: not disclosed

ARCHITECT: Zyscovich Architects

INTERIOR DESIGNER: Dennis Jenkins & Associates, Inc.

PHOTOGRAPHY: Lanny Provo
Nancy Robinson Watson

Something beyond mere material luxury is at hand when one visits Belvin and Lucille Friedson's residence. Situated amid lush foliage, the home's feeling of calm repose suggests the spirituality of its particular domesticity.

The contemporary, Japanese-inspired addition encompasses a master bedroom, library, bath and guest room that reflect the clients' cultural interests. The spare interior includes Japanese antiques, select woods, prized stones, fine silk fabrics and minimalist hardware. The window fenestrations allude to the East, and overlook

Oh, to unite home and nature

soulmates inseparable!

水 From the driveway's curves over the raised fertile land to the home itself, ensconcing a swimming pool and looking out toward a large pond beyond, the unity of landscape and structure, and the way both sit harmoniously on the land, promote an abundant flow of chi. That flow continues with the guest wing's sense of proportion and scale, its horizontal and vertical elements working in tandem with the architecture. Paintings, sculptures and floral arrangements are carefully placed throughout to orchestrate the flow of chi.

Japanese-inspired gardens. The shoji screens, when open, reveal the serene landscape beyond.

In the new wing, the elements predominate. Slate flooring and neutral color palette indicate the earth, as do the maple and mahogany cabinetry and chairs. The element of metal is present in the iron table. Mirrors, windows and shower enclosure symbolize water. Red accents in works of art and the bed treatment represent fire.

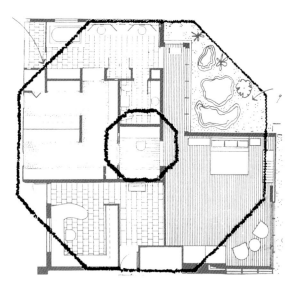

LOCATION: **Los Angeles, California**

SQUARE FEET/METERS: **6,000/557**

DESIGN BUDGET: **not disclosed**

ARCHITECT: **Toby Watson**

INTERIOR DESIGNER: **Maude MacGillivray Incorporated**

FENG SHUI CONSULTANT: **Janet Durovchic**

PHOTOGRAPHY: **Grey Crawford**

When author Janine Smith moved from a larger house to this smaller one, she was not as involved with feng shui as she is today. So architect Toby Watson produced an extensive remodel without feng shui as a guide. However, by the time Maude MacGillivray designed the interiors, Smith's interest in the ancient Chinese art of placement had grown.

A prime example is the walled exterior entry, seemingly custom designed for the later inclusion of artist Kurt Runstadler's glass-and-steel arches, installed to

Invite the fair winds to

*whisper to your soul*

soften the harsh river of chi aimed at the front door. Likewise, the interior indicates that a sensitivity intuitively in tune with feng shui was keenly expressed by MacGillivray.

Her custom-designed cabinetry organizes books and collectibles with a firm sense of order. Flexible lighting gives wings to Smith's ongoing pursuit of new expressions by talented artists. Various gathering places throughout invite one to sit and contemplate or entertain friends. The colors support Smith's spirited pursuit of creativity and knowledge.

風 In the living room, the television is covered by John Register's painting of a TV—a touch of visual wit. The library, appropriately located in the home's knowledge area according to the bagua map, is centered by Maude MacGillivray's clear maple table with black marble top and warmed by a patina of gold on the walls and a contemporary cast-stone fireplace. At the entry, various artworks, including five prints by Robert Mapplethorpe and a neon/wood/glass sculpture by Candice Gawne, create a sense of active serenity. In the master bedroom, feng shui's gray-blue tones symbolizing creativity are represented by a wealth of silk gauze, cotton and hand-printed linen velvet. In the master bathroom, rippled glass block welcomes light but preserves privacy, and maple cabinetry conveys the organic feeling of a classic Eames screen designed in the 1940s. In the guest powder room, a custom pullman in maple is topped by black marble embedded with fossils—a fitting homage to the client's environmental interests.

LOCATION: Pasig, Philippines

SQUARE FEET/METERS: 5,500/512

DESIGN BUDGET: $150,000

ARCHITECT/INTERIOR DESIGNER: Miller Yee Fong Architecture

PHOTOGRAPHY: Jose Campos III

Much of feng shui is as available to those who follow their innate sensibilities as to those who study the stars.

Wherever they have lived, the homeowners have always emphasized family gatherings with a host of friends. Harmony and laughter abound. So when they decided to build a new 5,500-square-foot residence on a 3,350-square-foot lot, they were able to bring as much to it as it could possibly give to them.

There were spiritual consultants, of course, since this is the Philippines. Their feng shui

# The home is where the

Worldly and sacred join.

木 Located in a densely packed urban area, the challenge was to get a large living space onto a small lot. The answer is a tall, thin four-story structure organized around an indoor garden that permeates all surrounding spaces with light, cross ventilation, nature and the sound of water from a Japanese *shi shi o doshi* fountain. The structure's east corner is cut top-to-bottom by a circular wall, a tribute to the morning sun that also balances the yang qualities of the straight, massive concrete building. Indigenous materials and artifacts are used throughout the house. Most of the wood, wrought iron and rattan furniture was designed by the architect and the owner, then manufactured at the client's own factory. Other surfaces are primarily concrete, stone and metal; wood is used sparingly in the Philippines due to termites. The living/dining area has been located along the home's west side, determined by the geomancer to be the site's major chi source.

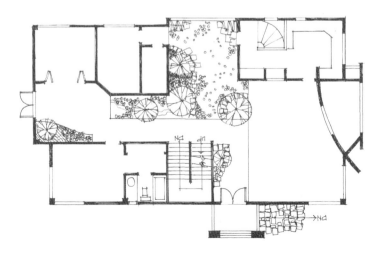

directives included not aligning door openings with each other, bathrooms with sleeping/living areas above, or orienting beds away from the door. The flow of chi was plotted with the aid of a geomancer's map and compass. The five feng shui elements were carefully balanced in and around the indoor garden.

Mainly, however, the light-filled four-story structure feels like an enchanted oasis due to the owner, a furniture manufacturer, and architect following their own intuitions—and the family's luminous spirit of togetherness. Theirs is a home where the sacred and the daily life mingle.

LOCATION: Montecito, California

SQUARE FEET/METERS: not disclosed

DESIGN BUDGET: not disclosed

INTERIOR DESIGNER: Feng Shui Design Associates

FENG SHUI CONSULTANT: Adele D. Trebil

PHOTOGRAPHY: Tom Burt/Jon Rouse

Dr. Jean-Marie Hamel, dean of a theological seminary, wanted to create an equally strong spiritual center for her private life.

Her home was already nurturing in many ways. However, its footprint, its floor plan, the balance of the elements and geopathogenic and electromagnetic zones needed fine-tuning to better support what she was seeking.

The central hallway aligned the front and back doors, creating a serious loss of chi. Thus furniture and leafy plants in an S-curve formation have been placed to deflect and slow chi along this

Beyond interior design lies

a bridge to pure essence.

土 Each section of the floor plan was checked for unbalanced energy placements and corrected with five-element energy placements. In the entry, where wood was determined to be too dominant, red (or fire) colored furnishings were specified. In the master bedroom, the bed was oriented toward a full view of the outside, its nurturing nature brought inside through lush plants. Also, their wood elements produce an environment that is energizing when combined with Hamel's predominantly fire trigram. An antique Asian print is used as a meditative mandala near the bed.

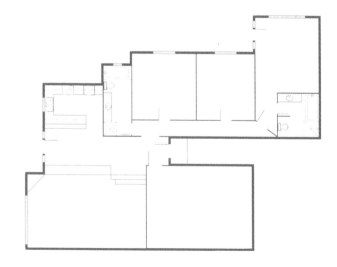

fast-paced pathway. Fountains also have been installed as chi accumulators to collect and then refract the energy back into the living space. Rounded upholstered pieces have been added to balance the architecture's angularity. And folk art and paintings that Hamel has collected or painted herself, along with gifts garnered through a lifetime of service, have been arranged to help unify her external and internal lives.

Other imbalances were also corrected through Classical Feng Shui, East-West Teaching, Black Hat ritual, electromagnetic testing, mitigation—and traditional prayer.

LOCATION: **Los Angeles, California**

SQUARE FEET/METERS: **2,500/232**

DESIGN BUDGET: **$78,000**

ARCHITECT/INTERIOR DESIGNER: **Feng Shui Architecture, Inc.**

FENG SHUI CONSULTANT: **Simona Mainini**

PHOTOGRAPHY: **Ogami/Burns, Pasadena**

Feng shui architect Simona Mainini knows that all "matter" is actually an illusion of reality—that everything physical is in fact energy vibrating at an individual frequency. And it is this understanding as well as good design that she tries to bring into people's lives.

In designing this home, she used her feng shui training to create a harmonious environment that incorporates her clients' collection of art and antiques.

In the front of the house Mainini created a screen of bamboo trees to avert a direct assault

The reality is energy,

matter is but an illusion.

of chi energy. In the backyard, she shaped and thinned an over-abundance of trees and plants that suffocated chi. She introduced water, in the form of a gently curving swimming pool, to absorb and store chi. To enhance the harmonious family life and relationship potential of the living room, she used an infusion of fire elements, including two large red Persian rugs, red paintings and candles.

These are but a few of the feng shui directives Mainini brought to the residence. She says they should be adjusted annually.

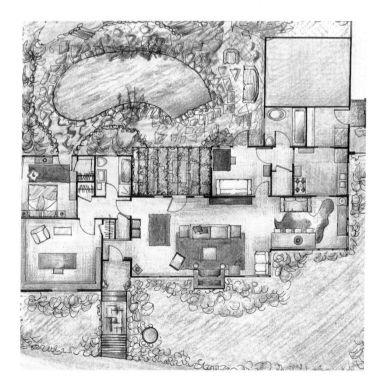

火 The ground is level around the entire property, enabling a constant, smooth flow of chi into the residence and its immediately surrounding area. The landscape is carefully tended to assure the right amount and quality of sunlight and chi flow gently into every room. In addition, the position of the furniture in each room is placed to be most effective according to this light and energy. For example, the desk overlooks the swimming pool, to the user's most energetic direction. Many of the owners' sacred Asian sculptures are placed in the dining room, where they become part of the view toward the protective bamboo screen. The location of the master bedroom has been changed to a smaller room with an enhanced view and a better magnetic field. To increase its positive earth energy, the fire element has been added in the form of an antique Persian rug. Light colors are used to offset the room's northern exposure, which does not get the greatest amount of sun.

LOCATION: São Paulo, Brazil

SQUARE FEET/METERS: 8,600/800

DESIGN BUDGET: not disclosed

ARCHITECT/INTERIOR DESIGNER: Sig Bergamin Arquitetura

FENG SHUI CONSULTANT: Harmonia de Ambientes

PHOTOGRAPHY: Tuca Reinés

Designer Sig Bergamin's life and work reflect a desire for calm.

For example, he used to allow himself to be caught up in the whirl of activities that comes with maintaining homes and offices in both Brazil and the United States. In recent years though, he has slowed the pace. "I aim over-all not for excitement, but for peace," he comments.

Even in his office environments, peace is the prevailing theme. This one, located in a two-story converted industrial building in São Paulo, encompasses 800 square meters filled

Be rid of nonessentials

and you gain the world!

with abundant natural light and lush greenery. The uncluttered space is filled with unadulterated white, the color Bergamin's feng shui consultant determined most fortuitous for his business. The result provides an ideal canvas against which to discuss clients' dreams unfettered by visual noise.

"I look at my surroundings as an avenue to rid myself of materialism," he says. "I want to concentrate more on people, on what's happening, on things more important than possessions can ever be."

金 Feng shui consultant Mariãngela Guimarães suggested the addition of some red objects to generate better relationships with his clients, as red symbolizes the element of fire, or warmth—as well as mirrors and pictures to fill the empty spaces and thus provide a greater sense of the symmetry so important in feng shui. She also felt that plants should be placed in the fireplace, because it is not used, to prevent chi energy from flying up the flue and to bring liveliness to an otherwise "dead" space. In addition, she relocated some offices in order to enhance their occupants' flux of energy.

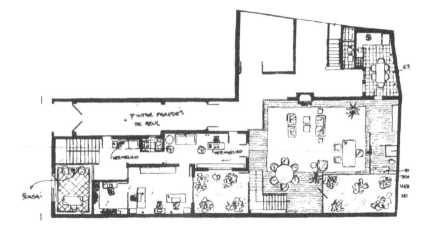

LOCATION: Los Gatos, California

SQUARE FEET/METERS: 1,800/167

DESIGN BUDGET: not disclosed

INTERIOR DESIGNER: Barbara Jacobs Interior Design

LIGHTING DESIGNER: LightSmiths Design Group

FENG SHUI CONSULTANT: Kathryn Metz

PHOTOGRAPHY: Russell MacMasters Photography

Already prominent in her field, interior designer Barbara Jacobs recently experienced a three-fold increase in her income and an elevated sense of health and harmony—much of which she credits to using feng shui.

Some design strategies she would have used anyway—replacing her living room's windows with 8-foot-high versions, using functional and flattering light throughout, and adding floor-to-ceiling shelving in the dining area for books and collectibles. But the fortuitous results are fundamental to feng shui.

A home's greatest stre

...ngths are rarely visible.

Then there were the decisions directed entirely by feng shui principles. These included locating a mirror over the fireplace, in the wealth corner of the bagua map, to prevent money from going up the chimney, and mirroring the wall behind the stove to allow rearview vision while cooking. In the bedrooms, she placed wiring in conduits for protection from the electrical field, covered beams to eliminate a sense of oppressiveness, and softened corners.

By addressing life's invisible as well as visible forces, Jacobs' home envelops her.

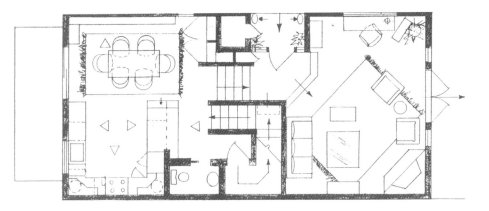

水 Warm woods such as mahogany and wenge and honed green marble create a sense of peace, harmony and warmth. Miniature light fixtures recessed under the cabinets provide task lighting without causing glare. Since the upstairs toilets were located almost directly over the entry and could allow good fortune to be flushed away, mirrors were installed face down under the subfloor to reflect good fortune back into the house. A mirrored niche was carved into the former entry wall so that it would no longer block chi. The bowl itself symbolically holds the owner's chi/life and, through recessed down lighting, is constantly illuminated. To make the master bedroom an ever welcoming spiritual retreat, the fireplace was highlighted with a pair of recessed, shielded fixtures to create the illusion of a roaring fire even when the fireplace is not in use. Opaque wall sconces behind the bed lend a further sense of warmth and security.

LOCATION: Pacific Palisades, California

SQUARE FEET/METERS: not disclosed

DESIGN BUDGET: $260,000

ENVIRONMENTAL DESIGNER: Dennis Stevens and Associates

PHOTOGRAPHY: ©1998 Jessica Z. Diamond

Designer Dennis Stevens has always desired to infuse people's lives with the joy that results from energy flowing freely between built and natural environments. So when he was introduced to feng shui, he took to it like a fish to water.

Stevens has used the principles of feng shui to further enhance his clients' living environments. This jewel of a home, the former residence of Dean Martin, has a panoramic view of the Riviera Country Club's entire golf course. Even so, its rear yard needed attention.

Nature's energy offers

*an infinity of joy.*

To induce a feeling of vital energy and auspicious capacity, Stevens enlarged the yard so he could place the pool far away from the house. He designed the pool with one curved edge that seems to extend the water into infinity.

The pool's size has been carefully calculated so that its proportions are suitable for this particular site. It fits naturally into its immediate landscape and does not detract from the existing positive force of energy.

No decks connect the pool to the house. Nature embraces residence and landscape as one.

風 For good fortune, the pool terrace faces southwest. All terraces are designed in irregular shapes, with corners softened by mock orange, Indian hawthorn, star jasmine, meyers asparagus and marthon II. Fine art from Asia and the Pacific Rim is placed throughout the landscape for a continuous, colorful and harmonious flow. As the plan indicates, the pool can be viewed as soon as one enters the house, thus immediately offering a sense of connection with the outdoors.

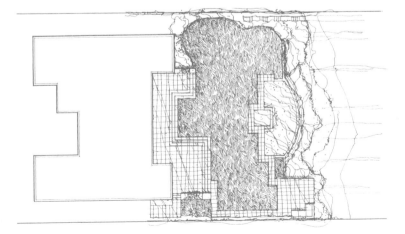

# Directory

Maude MacGillivray Incorporated
Maude MacGillivray
11022 Santa Monica Boulevard
Los Angeles, California 90025
Tel: (310) 479-1136
Fax: (310) 479-2174

## Architects and Interior Designers

**Alie Design Inc.**
Alie Chang
222 Amalfi Drive
Santa Monica, California 90402
Tel: (310) 459-1081
Fax: (310) 459-8530

**Barbara Jacobs Interior Design**
Barbara Jacobs, FASID
12340 Saratoga-Sunnyvale Road
Saratoga, California 95070
Tel: (408) 446-2225
Fax: (408) 446-2607

**Cheryl Rice Interiors**
Cheryl Rice
7460 Girard Avenue
La Jolla, California 92037
Tel/Fax: (619) 454-6223

**Cissie Cooper Design Services**
Cissie Cooper
4614 Mary Ellen Avenue
Sherman Oaks, California 91423
Tel: (818) 990-0525
Fax: (818) 990-4940

**Clodagh Design International**
Clodagh
Robert Pierpont
670 Broadway
New York, New York 10012
Tel: (212) 780-5300
Fax: (212) 780-5755

**David Ling Architect**
David Ling
110 East 17th Street
New York, New York 10003
Tel: (212) 982-7089
Fax: (212) 475-1336

**Dennis Jenkins & Associates, Inc.**
Dennis Jenkins
Diana Vogel
5813 SW 68th Street
South Miami, Florida 33143
Tel: (305) 665-6960
Fax: (305) 665-6971

**Dennis Stevens & Associates**
Dennis Stevens
8450 De Longpre Avenue
West Hollywood, California 90069
Tel: (213) 654-0425
Fax: (213) 654-2942

**Earth Design**
Jami Lin
P.O. Box 530725
Miami Shores, Florida 33153
Tel: (305) 756-6426
Fax: (305) 751-9995

**Feng Shui Architecture, Inc.**
Simona Mainini
289 South Robertson Boulevard
Beverly Hills, California 90211
Tel: (310) 772-8188
Fax: (310) 278-8869

**Feng Shui Design Associates**
Adele D. Trebil, President; CID,
FSI, Allied Member ASID
1355 Mistyridge Lane
Reno, Nevada 89503
Tel/Fax: (702) 746-4116

**Fletcher + Hardoin**
Daniel Fletcher
769 Pacific Street
Monterey, California 93940
Tel: (408) 373-5855
Fax: (408) 373-588

**Floss Barber Inc.**
Floss Barber
117 South 17th Street
Philadelphia, Pennsylvania 19103
Tel: (215) 557-0700
Fax: (215) 557-6700

**Hiatt Enterprises International, Inc.**
Douglas Pierce Hiatt,
ASID, IFDA, BVID
9454 Wilshire Boulevard
Beverly Hills, California 90212
Tel: (310) 275-5389
Fax: (310) 275-6890

**J.F. Chen Antiques**
Joel Chen
8414 Melrose Avenue
Los Angeles, California 90069
Tel: (213) 655-6310
Fax: (213) 655-9689

**Laura Bohn Design Associates, Inc.**
Laura Bohn
30 West 26th Street
New York, New York 10010
Tel: (212) 645-3636
Fax: (212) 645-3639

**LightSmiths Design Group**
Catherine Ng, IES
2145 19th Avenue
San Francisco, California 94116
Tel: (415) 682-0283
Fax: (415) 682-0285

**Luis Ortega Design Studio**
Luis Ortega
127 North Robertson Boulevard
Los Angeles, California 90211
Tel: (310) 358-0211
Fax: (310) 358-0221

**Maxcy Design**
Donald Maxcy
Marsha Maxcy
P.O. Box 5507
Carmel, California 93921
Tel: (831) 649-6582
Fax: (831) 649-6588

**Miller Yee Fong Architecture**
Miller Yee Fong
1500 Lombardy Road
Pasadena, California 91106
Tel: (626) 584-1190
Fax: (626) 577-4869

**Mitchell J. Rubin Associates, Inc.**
Mitchell J. Rubin
881 Seventh Avenue
New York, New York 10019
Tel: (212) 765-0801
Fax: (212) 765-0890

**Motoko Ishii Lighting Design, Inc.**
Motoko Ishii
Akari Lisa Ishii
5-4-11 Sendagaya, Shibuya-ku
Tokyo 151 Japan
Tel: (81) 3-3353-5311
Fax: (81) 3-3353-5120

**Carol Olten**
1335 Park Row
La Jolla, California 92037
Tel: (619) 454-3660

**Neiva Rizzotto**
Rua Sofia, 75 Jardim Europa
São Paulo, São Paulo 01447-030 Brazil
Tel: (55) 11-852-1977
Fax: (55) 11-282-1385

**Bonnie Sachs, ASID**
311 Bora Bora Way
Marina Del Rey, California 90292
Tel/Fax: (310) 306-4595

**Sig Bergamin Arquitetura**
Sig Bergamin
Rua Cônego Eugênio Leite 163
Jardim America
São Paulo, São Paulo 05414 Brazil
Tel: (55) 11-881-3433
Fax: (55) 11-3064-3490

**Steven Erhlich Architects**
Steven Ehrlich, FAIA
James Schmidt
10865 Washington Boulevard
Culver City, California 90232
Tel: (310) 838-9700
Fax: (310) 838-9737

**Studio Arthur de Mattos Casas**
Arthur de Mattos Casas
Al. Ministro Rocha Azevedo, 1052
São Paulo, São Paulo 01410-002 Brazil
Tel: (55) 11-282-6311
Fax: (55) 11-282-6608

**Thoryk Architecture, Inc.**
Paul Thoryk
1235 Shafter Street
San Diego, California 92106
Tel: (619) 523-9050
Fax: (619) 523-9035

**Toby Watson, Architect**
Toby Watson
205 Venice Way
Venice, California 90291
Tel: (310) 306-5095
Fax: (310) 578-6094

**Tokyo Misawa Homes, Inc.**
Hiroshi Mishiro
c/o Urban Design Architectural Office
3-19-11 Hamadayama
Suginami-ku, Tokyo 168 Japan
Tel: (81) 3-5378-3117
Fax: (81) 3-5378-3126

**Valerie von Sobel Interior Design**
Valerie von Sobel
P.O. Box 15427
Beverly Hills, California 90209
Tel: (310) 276-1572
Fax: (310) 276-1962

**Zyscovich Architects**
100 Biscayne Boulevard
Miami, Florida 33132
Tel: (305) 372-5222
Fax: (305) 577-4521

## Feng Shui Consultants

**Art of Placement**
Katherine Metz
602 Redstone Boulevard
Redstone, Colorado 81623
Tel: (970) 963-6688
Fax: (970) 963-6699

**Nathan V. Batoon**
3066 Mumford Avenue
Riverside, California 92503
Tel: (909) 353-8602

**Chun-Chia Hwang**
Tel: (626) 286-1099

**Durovchic & Associates**
Janet Durovchic
433 Town Center
Corte Madera, California 94925
Tel: (415) 924-9217
Fax: (415) 924-3315

**Earth Design**
Jami Lin
P.O. Box 530725
Miami Shores, Florida 33153
Tel: (305) 756-6426
(800) Earth Design
Fax: (305) 751-9995

**Feng Shui Solutions**
Kartar Diamond
P.O. Box 67354
Los Angeles, California 90067
Tel/Fax: (310) 820-7891

**Harmonia de Ambientes**
Mariãngela Guimarães
Renata Conde
Rua Almirante Tamandaré 66
Rio de Janeiro 22.210-060 Brazil
Tel/Fax: (55) 21-205-3000

**LCT Asssociates Ltd.**
Michael Chiang
Unit 4, 12/F, Eastern Harbour Centre
28 Hoi Chak Street
Quarry Bay, Hong Kong
Tel: (852) 2856-9389
Fax: (852) 2590-8672

**Paulo Lin**
Rua Luis Góes, 211
São Paulo, São Paulo 04043-40 Brazil
Tel: (55) 11-275-8118
Fax: (55) 11-5589-1809

**Lourdes Machado**
Rua Coronel Paulino Carlos, 174
São Paulo, São Paulo 04006-040 Brazil
Tel: (55) 11-884-3685
Fax: (55) 11-884-3685

**Simona Mainini**
289 South Robertson Boulevard
Beverlly Hills, California 90211
Tel: (310) 772-8188
Fax: (310) 278-8869

**The Metropolitan Institute of Interior Design**
Pamela Laurence, Allied Member
ASID, Executive Director
13 Newtown Road
Plainview, New York 11803
Tel: (516) 845-4033
Fax: (516) 845-8787

**Sarah Rossbach**
670 Broadway
New York, New York 10012
Tel: (212) 780-5300
Fax: (212) 780-5355

**Bonnie Sachs, ASID**
311 Bora Bora Way
Marina Del Rey, California 90292
Tel/Fax: (310) 306-4595

**Roy Anthony Shabla**
P.O. Box 4503
Downey, California 90241
Tel: (562) 927-3175

**Shuganshi Hidetada Takahashi**
4-24-24-204 Takanawa Minato-ku
Tokyo 108 Japan
Tel/Fax: (81) 3-3443-7386

**Tin Sun Metaphysics**
Master Pun Yin
8 Chatham Square
New York, New York 10038
Tel: (212) 285-0522
Fax: (212) 285-0523

**Western School of Feng Shui**
Terah Kathryn Collins
Jonathan Hulsh
437 South Highway 101
Solana Beach, California 92075
Tel: (619) 793-0945
(800) 300-6785
Fax: (619) 793-3499

**World Headquarters of Mankind's Greatest Knowledge/Potentialities**
Teck-Sing Tie
c/o Michaela Scherra and Associates
873 Cumberland Road
Glendale, California 91202
Tel: (818) 953-1503
Fax: (818) 240-2339

**Master Seann Xenja**
2344-B Silverado Trail
Napa, California 94558
Tel: (707) 226-2248
Fax: (707) 255-6306

## Photographers

**Barry J. Grossman Photography**
Barry Grossman
18224 SW 4 Court
Pembroke Pines, Florida 33029
Tel: (954) 433-5999
Fax: (954) 929-0430

**Catherine Tighe Bogert**
P.O. Box 89
Lambertville, New Jersey 08530
Tel/Fax: (609) 397-8966

**Brewster & Brewster**
Weldon Brewster
429½ California Street
Glendale, California 91203
Tel: (818) 956-3717
Fax: (818) 956-0530

**Campos Photography, Inc.**
Michael A. Campos
4879 Ronson Court
San Diego, California 92111
Tel: (619) 715-8150
Fax: (619) 715-8152

**Jose Campos III**
9 Banaba Circle
Makati, Forbes Philippines
Tel: (632) 817-7505
Fax: (632) 810-6156

**Charles White Photography**
Charles S. White
154 North Mansfield Avenue
Los Angeles, California 90036
Tel: (213) 937-3117
Fax: (213) 937-1808

**Daniel Aubry Studio**
Daniel Aubry
100 West 23rd Street
New York, New York 10011
Tel: (212) 414-0014
Fax: (212) 414-0013

**Five Star Productions**
Tom Burt
Jon Rouse
479 El Sueno
Santa Barbara, California 93105
Tel: (805) 683-0464
Fax: (805) 692-9827

**Grey Crawford Photography**
Grey Crawford
2924 Park Center Drive
Los Angeles, California 90068
Tel: (213) 413-4299
Fax: (213) 851-4252

**Ichigaya Studio**
Yoichi Yamazaki
72-8 Yakuoji-cho, Ichigaya
Shinjuku-ku, Tokyo 162 Japan
Tel: (81) 3-3235-1490
Fax: (81) 3-3235-1492

**Image Center**
Marco Zecchin
1219 Willo Mar Drive
San Jose, California 95118
Tel: (408) 723-3649
Fax: (408) 723-0114

**Jessica Z. Diamond Photography**
Jessica Z. Diamond
14004-B Marquesas Way
Marina del Rey, California 90292
Tel: (310) 827-7993
Fax: (310) 827-0011

**Lanny Provo Photography**
Lanny Provo
100 NE 101 Street
Miami Shores, Florida 33138
Tel/Fax: (305) 756-0136

**Martin Fine Photography Inc.**
Martin Fine
11019 Limerick Avenue
Chatsworth, California 91311
Tel/Fax: (818) 341-7113

**Mauricio Simonetti
Fotografia Ltda. ME**
Mauricio Simonetti
Rua Afonso Celso, 131/25
São Paulo, São Paulo 04119-000 Brazil
Tel/Fax: (55) 11-575-2917

**Michael Dunne
Photography & Design**
Michael Dunne
54 Stokenchurch Street
London SW6 3TR England
Tel: (44) 171-736-6171
Fax: (44) 171-731-8792

**Misawa Homes Co., Ltd.**
Yoshinori Komatsu
2-4-1 Nishi-Shinjuku
Shinjuku-ku, Tokyo Japan
Tel: (81) 3-3345-1111
Fax: (81) 3-5381-7833

**Mary E. Nichols**
232 North Arden Boulevard
Los Angeles, California 90004
Tel: (213) 871-0770
Fax: (213) 871-0775

**NRW**
Nancy Robinson Watson
609 Ocean Drive
Key Biscayne, Florida 33149
Tel: (305) 361-9182
Fax: (305) 361-6791

**Ogami/Burns**
Gene Ogami
500 South Raymond
Pasadena, California 91105
Tel: (626) 796-3248

**Carol Olten**
1335 Park Row
La Jolla, California 92037
Tel: (619) 454-3660

**Jerry Rife**
5645 Guincho Court
San Diego, California 92112
Tel: (619) 292-0117

**Ron Starr Photography**
Ron Starr
4104 24th Street
San Francisco, California 94114
Tel: (415) 541-7732
Fax: (415) 285-9518

**Russell Abraham Photography**
Russell Abraham
60 Federal Street
San Francisco, California 94107
Tel: (415) 896-6400
Fax: (415) 896-6402

**Russell MacMasters & Associates**
Russell MacMasters
860½ De Haro Street
San Francisco, California 94107
Tel: (415) 824-0800
Fax: (415) 285-7003

**RVC Produções e Studio de
Fotografia Ltda.**
Ricardo de Vicq de Cumptich
Rua Pedro Teixeira, 91 Vila Olimpia
São Paulo, São Paulo 04550-010 Brazil
Tel: (55) 11-866-1104
Fax: (55) 11-828-0085

**Tim Street-Porter**
2074 Watsonia Terrace
Los Angeles, California 90068
Tel: (323) 874-4278
Fax: (213) 876-8795

**Todd Eberle Photography**
Todd Eberle
54 West 21st Street
New York, New York 10010
Tel: (212) 243-2511
Fax: (212) 243-3587

**Tom Crane Photography Inc.**
Tom Crane
Jeff Totaro
113 Cumberland Place
Bryn Mawr, Pennsylvania 19010
Tel: (610) 525-2444
Fax: (610) 527-7529

**Tuca Reinés Estudio Fotográfico**
Tuca Reinés
Rua Emanuel Kant, 58
São Paulo, São Paulo 04536-050 Brazil
Tel: (55) 11-3061-9127
Fax: (55) 11-852-8735

**Wade Zimmerman**
9 East 97th Street
New York, New York 10029
Tel: (212) 427-8784
Fax: (212) 427-3526

# Index

# Afterword

*And so we have seen that feng shui is always moving and changing. Architects, designers, and master feng shui consultants, forever intuitive and inspired, express it this way:*

The environment reflects the dweller; the dweller affects the environment. To the unrealized, they appear as two; to the realized, they are always one —**Teck-Sing Tie, Vice-Chairman, Prime Knowledge and Potential Center, Malaysia** Beyond interior design there is feng shui. Beyond feng shui there is that eternal realm pure essence—spirit, energy. Feng shui is a bridge that connects us to this realm.—**Adele D. Trebil, CID, FSI, Allied Member ASID; President, Feng Shui Design Associates, Reno, Nevada** My house has become a form that houses the essence of what I embody.—**Dr. Jean-Marie Hamel, Montecito, California, client of Adele D. Trebil** Feng shui can empower your life by designing according to its concepts through personal symbolism and your personal style.—**Jami Lin, Earth Design, Miami Shores, Florida** By integrating feng shui in the design process, the requirements of client, site, architecture and the natural environment are balanced—and beauty and harmony can be achieved.—**Bonnie Sachs, ASID, Certified Interior Designer and Feng Shui Consultant, Los Angeles, California** Based on the concepts of yin and yang, feng shui includes every element in our universe.— **Chun-Chia Hwang, Feng Shui Consultant, Pasadena, California** Many times sensitive people not trained about the principles of feng shui still use them automatically—just by listening to the silence within us.—**Valerie von Sobel, Interior Designer, Los Angeles, California** Feng shui and good design are usually synonymous. Both arts involve color, lighting, views, furniture arrangement, textures, and a practical functionality of space. What is not obvious is that feng shui transcends our aesthetic sense.—**Kartar Diamond, Feng Shui Consultant, Los Angeles, California** As a designer, I cannot imagine one's immediate surroundings not empowering one toward a better attitude, therefore a better life.—**Dennis Jenkins, Dennis Jenkins & Associates, South Miami, Florida** Until I used feng shui, my work was limited to creating a soothing atmosphere, a sanctuary where my clients would be comforted by their surroundings. Now with the help of feng shui, my clients can shift to higher ground and prosper in every area of their lives.— **Cissie Cooper, Cissie Cooper Design Services, Sherman Oaks, California** Feng shui is not a fad—it has had value for thousands of years.— **Sarah Rossbach, Feng Shui Consultant, New York City, New York** As a writer on interior design, I have developed a great deal of curiosity about feng shui.—**Carol Olten, Journalist/Designer, La Jolla, California** Feng shui brings to the West the comfort, safety and beauty of mindful design. It honors our basic needs to be nurtured and inspired by our homes and work places, bridging our quality of life with our physical environments.—**Terah Kathryn Collins, Founder, Western School of Feng Shui, Solana Beach, California** It is not that lucky houses make lucky people, it is that lucky people end up living in lucky houses.—**Miller Yee Fong, Architect, Pasadena, California** Here in Brazil, as in the rest of the world, feng shui is becoming a mania.—**Mariàngela Guimarães, Harmonia de Ambientes, Rio de Janeiro, Brazil** It should be a constant discipline and practice to eliminate and to process things not essential or meaningful to us personally, so our precious space will not be choked by things that blur our mental clarity and clutter our physical space.—**Alie Chang, Alie Design, Inc., Santa Monica, California** Feng shui utilizes our environment as a "magic" mirror of ourselves.—**Pamela Laurence, Allied Member ASID, Executive Director, The Metropolitan Institute of Interior Design, Plainview, New York** In feng shui philosophy, the house, like the owner/occupant that uses it, has a life cycle of its own. The house has a cycle of "birth-growth-maturity-disease-death" and this varies from house to house.—**Michael Chiang, LCT Associates Ltd., Hong Kong and Shanghai, China** The West is so receptive to the practice of feng shui that it seems likely that in a hundred years we will be able to teach the East.—**Neiva Gessi Rizzotto, Landscape Designer, São Paulo, Brazil** Properly applied, feng shui helps to balance the energy flow in our environment, enabling us to take advantage of energetic, healthy and harmonious houses.—**Simona Mainini**